F-16
Fighting Falcon

F-16
Fighting Falcon

Roy Braybrook

OSPREY
AEROSPACE

Published in 1991 by Osprey Publishing
Limited, 59 Grosvenor Street, London
W1X 9DA

ISBN 1–85532–150–5

Edited by Tony Holmes
Designed by Paul Kime
Printed in Hong Kong

Front cover Slowly closing on the flying
boom, the pilot of this Royal Netherlands
Air Force F-16B has already opened the
refuelling receptacle door on the spine of
his aircraft. Serialled J-264 and hailing from
No 322 Sqn at Leeuwarden, this airframe is
just one of 213 Fighting Falcons bought by
the Dutch since 1979. Regular customers
for the USAFE tanker force, the RNAF
F-16s could soon be refuelling from their
own KC-10 Extenders as the Dutch have
decided that they need their own air-to-air
tanking capability (*Robbie Shaw*)

Back cover The warm camouflage colours
worn by these F-16s contrast markedly with
the more standard USAF tactical greys.
Assigned to *Grupo de Caza* 16 of the *Fuerzas
Aereas Venezolanas*, the aircraft are the only
examples of the nimble General Dynamics
fighter so far sold to any South American
country, 18 single seaters and six twins
being delivered to Maracay airbase in late
1983 (*Peter R Foster*)

Half title page The F-16 is now in service
with the USAF, ANG, AFRES, US Navy, and
15 overseas air forces. This example is one
of a force of 70 F-16A/Bs purchased by the
Royal Danish Air Force (*Ian Black*)

Title page The Fighting Falcon now
provides much of the USAF's frontline
fighter strength. This F-16A (81–0737) was
photographed at RAF Finningley in 1985, its
'HR' tail-code showing that it hailed from
the 50th TFW based at Hahn AFB in
Germany, and its blue fin-stripe indicating
membership of the 10th TFS. The wing now
has the F-16C, and this aircraft is currently
in storage, pending re-assignment to the
ANG (*Duncan Cubitt/Airforces Monthly*)

Contents

The most populous fast jet in Europe, the
Fighting Falcon performs all manner of tasks
within NATO. This shark-mouthed F-16C,
for example, is a radar-busting Wild Weasel
from the 52nd Tactical Fighter Wing.
Normally based at Spangdahlem, in
Germany, this aircraft has just arrived at
Boscombe Down, in Hampshire, for the
1990 Battle of Britain Airshow weekend.
The tri-colour stripes and the '52nd TFW'
titling on the fin mark this airframe as the
wing commander's personal mount
(*Tony Holmes*)

USAFE/PACAF Fighting Falcons

The General Dynamics (GD) F-16 Fighting Falcon has been one of the great success stories of American aviation, not only in a technological sense, but also as a commercial programme and in terms of the military results that it has achieved in various conflicts.

Preliminary design work began in 1968, but the project only took off in April 1972, when GD and Northrop were chosen by the USAF Aeronautical Systems Division at Wright-Patterson AFB to build technology demonstrators for a future lightweight fighter (LWF). The first of these prototypes into the air was GD's YF-16 (serial 72–01567), which had its maiden flight on 2 February 1974, and was joined in the flight test programme by the second YF-16 (72–01568) on 9 May 1974. The two Northrop YF-17s came some weeks later. Then the USAF decided to cut the flight tests short, and changed this research programme into a two-horse race for the new air combat fighter (ACF).

On 13 January 1975 the GD aircraft was chosen for its superior performance, lower cost, and engine commonality with the F-15 that it was to complement. The first of six full-scale development (FSD) aircraft (serials 75–0745 to –0750) had its maiden flight on 8 December 1976, and by June 1978 the whole batch was flying, plus two FSD two-seaters (75–0751 and –0752). By July 1990 no less than 1482 F-16A/Bs and 1201 F-16C/Ds had been delivered. Firm orders from 17 services stood at an incredible 3765 aircraft, and on current plans this number will increase to at least 4764.

The technologies employed in this outstandingly successful design included wing-body blending, forebody strakes for controlled vortex lift, automatic leading edge manoeuvre flaps, an underslung intake for operations at high angles, a high visibility, high-G cockpit with sidestick and fly-by-wire (FBW) controls making possible an aircraft that is longitudinally unstable in subsonic flight at low angles of attack (AOA). The combined result was a quantum leap in air combat effectiveness.

Unusually dramatic lighting for this F-16A (80–0613) from the 10th TFS/50th TFW, landing at RAF Alconbury in 1984 just ahead of a thunderstorm. Note the unit badges on the intake duct and the countershaded camouflage. From June 1978 USAF (and most other) F-16s have been painted dark grey (Federal Standard 36081) in what is termed the 'saddle area', middle grey (FS 36118) on the front fuselage and vertical tail, and underbelly grey (FS 36375) on the undersurfaces. Having returned to the USA this Fighting Falcon now sallies forth with an ANG posterior in the 'saddle', the aircraft assigned to the 182nd TFS at Kelly AFB, Texas (*Peter R Foster*)

The importance of the F-16 is reflected in its frontline deployment in Europe and the Pacific, although some of these units will probably be taken back to the US following the thawing of the Cold War. Within USAFE the 17th Air Force in Germany includes the 50th TFW at Hahn AB, the 86th TFW at Ramstein AB, and the 52nd TFW at Spangdahlem AB, whilst the 16th Air Force in Spain continues to exercise control over the 401st TFW at Torrejon AB until 1992 when the wing is scheduled to move to Italy . The 3rd Air Force in the UK also controls the 81st TFW at RAF Bentwaters/Woodbridge, which until early 1990 included F-16s with the 527th Aggressor Sqn. Within PACAF the 7th Air Force in Korea has F-16s with the 8th TFW at Kunsan AB and the 51st TFW at Osan AB, whilst the 5th Air Force in Japan has F-16s with the 432nd TFW at Misawa AB.

The military success of the F-16 might be summarized in the 50 to zero kill ratio believed to have been achieved by Israeli and Pakistani F-16s against Soviet-built fighters. However, equally significant was the strike by Israeli F-16s against Iraq's nuclear facility near Baghdad in June 1981, carrying heavy bombloads over a radius in excess of 500 nm (925 km). Although intended originally as a lightweight dogfight aircraft, the F-16 has clearly developed into a remarkably versatile fighter-bomber, and the latest equipment fit has extended its effectiveness into night-time operations.

Right Nose art is not often seen on F-16s, but this example was recorded at RAF Mildenhall in 1988, the canvas being F-16C serial 84–1298 from the 10th TFS/50th TFW, based at Hahn AB (*T Malcolm English*)

Above A fine portrait of F-16C serial 84–1298 from the 10th TFS 50th/TFW at Coxyde in Belgium in 1987. The falcon on the fin has appeared on Hahn F-16s since the mid 1980s. The blister on the nose just aft of the radome covers one of the antennas of the radar-warning receiver (RWR), which in this Block 25/30 aircraft would be an Applied Technology/Dalmo Victor ALR-69 (*Bob Archer*)

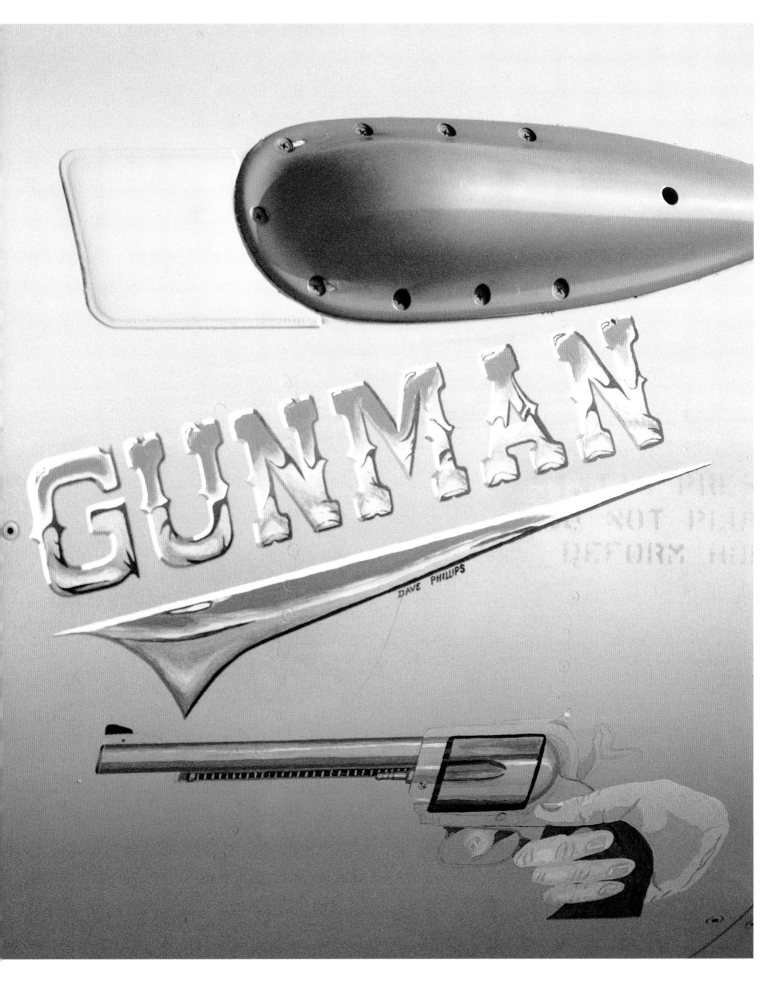

A representative of the 50th TFW (about to land at RAF Lakenheath in 1989), this example (84–1306) bears the yellow fin stripe with black outline of the 496th TFS. The aircraft pictured is fitted with AIM-9L Sidewinders on stations one and nine, plus 308 Imp gal (1400 litre) tanks on stations four and six, and practice weapons carriers on stations three and seven (*Bob Archer*)

One of General Dynamics' exhibits at Farnborough 1990 was an F-16C borrowed from the 86th TFW at Ramstein AB in Germany, and equipped to 'Night Falcon' standard. Seen here being towed out for static display early one morning during the show, the F-16 wears the red and black diagonal fin-stripes which mark it as a member of the 526th TFS of the 86th TFW, the other squadron being the 512th TFS, with green and black diagonal fin-stripes. This F-16C, serial 85–1446, is a Block 30/32 aircraft with a 'configured' engine bay, allowing it to take either the original P&W F100 or GE's F110. In fact, GD representatives at Farnborough indicated that this aircraft has the 25,418 lb (11,530 kg) F110-GE–100, which narrows it down to a Block 30. The corresponding Block 32 has the 23,830 lb (10,800 kg) F100-PW–220. For the show this aircraft was equipped with the Martin Marietta Lantirn (Low Altitude Navigation and Targeting Infra-Red for Night) pods on intake stations 5L and 5R, although full Lantirn provisions were introduced only with Block 40/42 aircraft, beginning October/November of 1988 (*Tony Holmes*)

A close-up of the impressive armament
carried by the Farnborough 1990 F-16C.
AIM-9L/Ms were carried on stations one,
two, eight and nine and Hughes AGM-65
Mavericks were loaded on triple launch
racks on stations three and seven. The
USAF employs both the TV-guided
AGM-65A/B and the imaging infra-red
AGM-65D/G. In either case the missile
produces a TV-like image on a cockpit
display, and the pilot selects the target and
launches the missile, after which guidance is
automatic. The A/B/D versions deliver a
125 lb (56.7 kg) warhead, but in the case of
the -65D this weight is being increased to
300 lbs (136 kgs). Due to the use of IR
homing, the AGM-65D can be used at night,
whereas TV guidance is generally restricted
to daylight operations (*T Malcolm English*)

A brightly painted representative of the 86th TFW, photographed in 1986, and presumably the wing's display aircraft for that season. The wing insignia is repeated toned-down on the intake (*Ian Black*)

Below The personal mount of the 526th TFS commander, F-16C 85–1426 has had some of the serial digits enlarged to promote squadron identity and the vertical tail has been decorated for display purposes. It was pictured at Ramstein outside its hardened aircraft shelter (HAS) in 1987 (*Peter R Foster*)

Left One of three F-16Ds operated by the 52nd TFW at Spangdahlem AB in Germany, serial 86–0042 comes in to land at RAF Mildenhall in 1988. The yellow fin-stripe outlined in black denotes membership of the 81st TFS. The black underwing stores probably contains nothing more sinister than a set of golf clubs and a dress shirt and trousers! (*Duncan Cubitt/Airforces Monthly*)

Above This F-16C, serial 87–0257, appeared at RAF Alconbury in 1989, its dark blue fin-stripe outlined in white indicating the 23rd TFS. The third squadron of the 52nd TFW is the 480th, which has a red fin-stripe. All three squadrons operate a mix of F-16C/Ds and F-4G 'Wild Weasels', the latter detecting, locating and attacking hostile radars, while the Fighting Falcons presumably fly escort. A dedicated 'Wild Weasel' version of the F-16 has been proposed, but for economy reasons no decision has yet been taken on replacing the F-4G (*Peter R Foster*)

Right Rear end of F-16C serial 86–0341 on detachment from the 401st TFW, based at Torrejon in Spain, to Incirlik AB in Turkey in 1989. The black and yellow chequered fin-stripe is for the 613th TFS. The Sidewinder is clearly only an acquisition round, since the wings lack the wind-driven gyros that control the ailerons and provide the missile with roll stability. Elements of the 401st spent quite some time at Incirlik during *Operation Desert Storm*, the USAF opening up a second front into Iraq from the Turkish base. Other Torrejon F-16s flew further afield to Doha International Airport in Qatar, these Fighting Falcons mainly flying sorties into occupied Kuwait (*Duncan Cubitt/Airforces Monthly*)

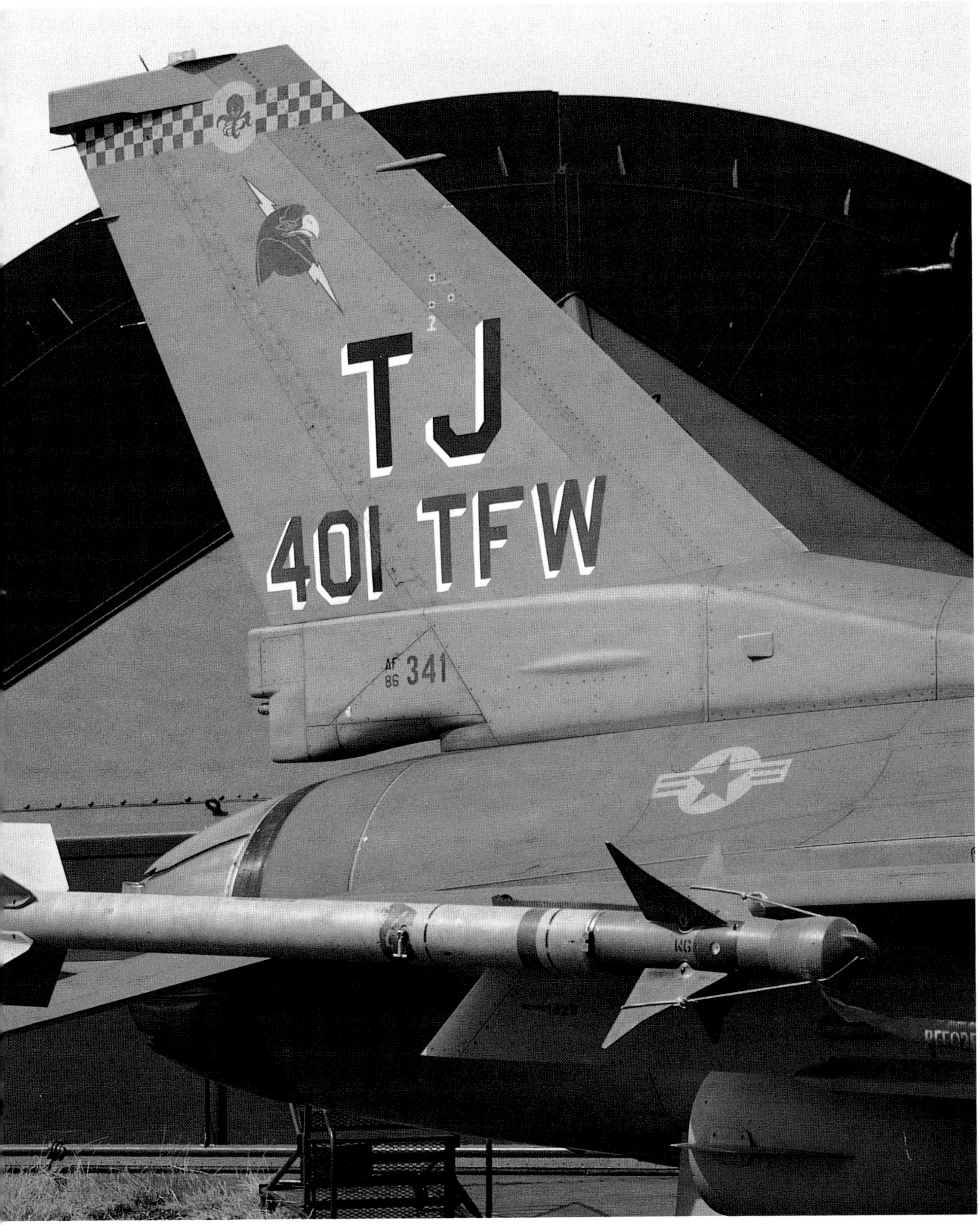
TJ
401 TFW
AF 86 341

Above A flight of 401st TFW F-16Cs on the 1989 Incirlik detachment, with various provisions for practice bombs and rocket projectiles. The wing consists of three squadrons; the 612th, 613th and 614th, distinguished by blue and white, yellow and black, and red and white chequered fin-stripes respectively. The 401st TFW is due to leave Spain in 1991, and initial plans call for its redeployment to Crotone AB in southern Italy, though the wing may yet be disbanded as an economy measure (*Duncan Cubitt/Airforces Monthly*)

Above right For a short period the F-5Es of the 527th Aggressor Sqn, based at RAF Alconbury, were replaced by F-16Cs of the same unit at RAF Bentwaters, the Fighting Falcons thus becoming part of the 81st TFW. However, the 527th TFTAS was deactivated in early 1990. This photograph shows F-16C serial 85–1479 with –1453 in the background, both at RAF Bentwaters in late 1988. Note the toned-down fin insignia in the form of a rampant bear (*Bob Archer*)

Below right This F-16C (serial 86–0207) from the famous 'Wolf Pack' 8th TFW was pictured at Kunsan AB in South Korea in October 1987. Its fin bears the PACAF shield, the wolf's head insignia of the wing and the blue stripe indicating membership of the 35th TFS. When the F-16 was first introduced, one of the features that brought most comments from observers was the way its tailplane constantly moved as the aircraft rolled over the ground, its flight control system sensing the bumps and automatically trying to iron out the runway (*Peter R Foster*)

Right This slightly earlier photograph, taken in March 1987, shows one of the F-16As (80–0578) that previously equipped the wing. The yellow fin-stripe is for the 80th TFS ('Headhunters'). This rear quarter shot illustrates the neat airbrake design, which probably gives no pitching moment on extension, and allows the brakes to be left open throughout the landing. As with most surviving 8th TFW F-16As, this particular aircraft was passed onto the 347th TFW at Moody AFB in Georgia in early 1988 (*Robbie Shaw*)

Above The blue and yellow fin-stripe and the fact that the pilot is a full colonel suggest that this is the personal transportation of the commander of the 8th TFW. It is pictured during a 1985 visit to Kadena AB, Okinawa, alongside an F-4 and A-10 in dedicated mud-moving colours. One of the first overseas wings to receive the F-16, the 8th TFW traded in their venerable F-4Ds for brand new A-model Fighting Falcons in later 1981. Whilst the F-4D performed the primary close air support mission, the F-16 is assigned to battlefield air interdiction and deep strike, retaining its 'swing-force' capability to perform effectively in the air defence role (*Bob Archer*)

Based in America

Despite the large numbers of USAF F-16s deployed in Europe and the Pacific, TAC retains six full-scale F-16 wings within the CONUS (Continental United States) area, and there are many smaller units equipped (in whole or in part) with this highly flexible fighter. Within TAC's 9th Air Force, headquartered at Shaw AFB, South Carolina, there are F-16s with the 31st TFW at Homestead AFB, Florida; the 56th Tactical Training Wing at MacDill AFB, Florida; the 347th TFW at Moody AFB, Georgia; and the 363rd TFW at Shaw AFB. On a smaller scale, within the 12th Air Force, headquartered at Bergstrom AFB, Texas, there are F-16s with the 58th Tactical Training Wing at Luke AFB, Arizona; the 388th TFW at Hill AFB, Utah; and the 57th Fighter Weapons Wing, which includes the Air Demonstration Sqn or simply the 'Thunderbirds'.

By General Dynamics' count, aside from the hundreds of F-16s employed by the ANG and AFRES units, there are Fighting Falcons to be found with Air Force Systems Command (AFSC) at Edwards AFB Air Force Flight Test Center (AFFTC), and with AFSC's Aeronautical Systems Division at Wright-Patterson AFB, Ohio (YF-1) and at Griffiss AFB, New York (YF-2). Others are to be found at the USAF Academy (USAFA) in Colorado Springs, at Air Force Logistics Command's Ogden Air Logistics Center (ALC) in Utah, at Sentile AFB in Ohio, at Lowry AFB in Colorado, and at Sheppard AFB in Texas.

In a nose-count dated 30 September 1989, the USAF had on charge a total of 977 F-16s with an average age of 3.6 years, while the ANG had 338 F-16A/Bs averaging 7.6 years, and AFRES units had 118 averaging 8.0 years. The total was thus 1433 F-16s at that time.

In addition to these numbers (which include USAFE and PACAF aircraft), the US Navy has purchased 26 F-16C/Ds under the designation F-16N for use in adversary training programmes at three CONUS bases: NAS Miramar, California; NAS Key West, Florida; and NAS Oceana, Virginia.

The unique operational flexibility and long range of the F-16 mean that CONUS-based units are well suited to the rapid reinforcement of overseas actions. This was demonstrated by the deployment of F-16s from the 363rd TFW at Shaw AFB in South Carolina to Sharjah in the United Arab Emirates (UAE) during the early days of the Gulf crisis in 1990, the wing becoming heavily involved in *Operation Desert Storm*, which began in January 1991.

Left Photographed while taking part in a Red Flag attack sortie from Nellis AFB in 1985, this 56th TTW F-16 appears to be carrying a centreline 250 Imp gal (1135 litre) tank, an AIM-9L on the starboard wingtip, an air combat manoeuvring instrumentation (ACMI) data pod on the port tip and four Mk 81 bombs, each weighing a nominal 250 lb (113 kg). Its blue fin-stripe, outlined in white, denotes that this F-16 belongs to the 62nd TFTS (*Frank B Mormillo*)

Above left Cat's eye view of an F-16C of the 56th Tactical Training Wing (TTW), seen visiting London, Ontario, in 1990. The black 'Panthers' fin-stripe identifies it as belonging to the 72nd TFTS, one of four squadrons within the 56th TTW. The 61st, 62nd, 63rd and 72nd TFTSs operate between them 11 A-models, 3 B-models, 50 C-models and 34 D-models, thus making the 56th TTW the second largest owner of F-16s in the USA. It is based at MacDill AFB, near Tampa, Florida, the airfield being activated in 1941 and named after Col Leslie MacDill who died in a flying accident in 1938 (*Robbie Shaw*)

Below left This F-16B (serial 78–0099) of the 56th TTW was photographed at MacDill AFB in 1981, its yellow fin-stripe showing its assignment to the 61st TFTS. The 'scene mag' Maverick under the wing is a Hughes AGM-65B TV-guided missile, in which the camera's field of view is reduced to 2.5 degrees, half that of the AGM-65A, and gives increased target acquisition range. Weight is unchanged at 462 lbs (210 kgs) (*Robbie Shaw*)

Above This landing shot of an F-16C (serial 83–1122) shows an aircraft of the 58th TTW, bearing the black fin-stripe of the 312th TFTS. This early Block 25 aircraft was in fact the fifth production F-16C. Currently the biggest Fighting Falcon unit in the USA, the wing operates two squadrons of F-16A/Bs (the 310th and 311th TFTS) and two equipped with the F-16C/D (the 312th and 314th). Luke AFB is the largest fighter training base in the world, with courses for USAF and foreign pilots on the F-16, F-15 and F-15E. The base was activated in 1941 and was named after Second Lt Frank Luke Jr, a World War I pilot with an impressive record of destroying observation balloons. Luke was the first pilot to receive the Medal of Honor and was killed in action in France in 1918 (*Milslides via Bob Archer*)

Below An interesting example of the 58th TTW's training of overseas pilots is provided by this F-16B which bears the 'LF' tail-code and the USAF serial 87–0402, but is actually part of a batch of four F-16As and four F-16Bs (serials 87–0397 to –0404) purchased by the Republic of Singapore Air Force. Training was carried out by the USAF at Luke AFB, where this photograph was taken in October 1988, before delivery to Singapore. The red fin-stripe contains the RSAF insignia within its borders, this small marking being the aircraft's only distinguishing feature (*Peter R Foster*)

Right This late production F-16B (serial 82–1026) bears the 'MY' tail-code of the 347th TFW and the blue and white chequered stripe of the 70th TFS. The wing insignia is just visible on the intake duct, and it is carrying practice bombs on the outer pylons. The 347th is based at Moody AFB in Georgia, an airfield that was opened in 1941 and named after Major James P Moody who was killed in the previous year while test-flying the Beech AT-10 (*Milslides via Bob Archer*)

This F-16A (serial 81–0703) was also a member of the 70th TFS when it was photographed landing at the Georgia base in 1988. Now a 'weekend warrior,' the aircraft has since been upgraded to Air Defence Fighter (ADF) specs and issued to the 111th FIS at Ellington ANGB in Texas. One of the few pilot criticisms made of the F-16 is that it is difficult to land smoothly, partly due to its extremely stiff landing gear which gives a sensation of bouncing at touchdown, even if the wheels are still on the ground. Inexperienced pilots are thus encouraged to make sidestick inputs, and may overcontrol. The F-16 employs an approach angle of either 11 or 13 degrees, and is landed at an AOA of 13 degrees (restricted by ground clearance at the rear end). View over the nose is such that the touchdown point can be seen with the aircraft in landing attitude (*Milslides via Bob Archer*)

This F-16C (serial 84–1253) bears the 'SW' tail-code of the 363rd TFW, based at Shaw AFB, South Carolina, but was seen visiting Canada in 1990. The white fin-stripe denotes the 17th TFS, which was traditionally known as 'Owls', but appears to have been renamed 'Hooters'. The other squadrons are the 19th TFS ('Gamecocks'), and the 33rd TFS ('Falcons'). The base was inaugurated in 1941 and named after Second Lt Ervin D Shaw, who was shot down over France just before the end of World War 1 while performing a reconnaissance sortie in a Bristol Fighter. The Fighting Falcons of the 363rd were some of the first aircraft to be deployed to the Gulf at the commencement of *Operation Desert Shield*. A total of 44 aircraft from the 17th and 33rd TFSs were despatched to Sharjah, in the United Arab Emirates, on 8 August, and at least 16 C-5 Galaxy flights were made in support of this deployment, carrying maintenance and support personnel. The 507th Tactical Air Control Wing, together with its deployable communications and radar equipment (plus ground-based forward air controllers) also deployed from Shaw. The 'Hooters' and the 'Falcons' were heavily involved in the massive air assault against Iraq's Republican Guard during *Desert Storm*, using both Rockeyes and Mavericks to great effect against dug-in emplacements (*Robbie Shaw*)

Overleaf Typical tanker shot of the F-16, in this case a member of the 388th TFW (tail-code 'HL') and the 4th TFS, which is indicated by a yellow fin-stripe with a black lightning bolt. The wing's other two squadrons are the 34th TFS ('Rams') and the 421st TFS ('Black Widows'). As with the 363rd TFW, two squadrons from the 388th were sent to the Gulf to bolster the ranks just prior to *Desert Storm* commencing. The 388th is based at Hill AFB in Utah, an airfield that began operations in 1940 and was named after Major Ployer P Hill who died on 30 October 1935 while test-flying the first B-17 (*Paul F Crickmore*)

Above These F-16As (79–0394 and –0407) date back to the second year of production procurement, and were photographed in 1981 taking off at Nellis AFB, Nevada, for a practice bombing sorties. Assigned the 'NA' code of the 474th TFW, they were transferred elsewhere when the Nellis-based wing was deactivated in 1989 due to budget restrictions. The aircraft (both from the 430th TFS) are shown carrying an AGM-65A/B TV-guided Maverick under the right wing and a practice weapons carrier under the left, the latter store having provisions for four 2.75 inch (70 mm) folding-fin aircraft rockets (FFARs) in addition to the four small practice bombs (*Frank B Mormillo*)

Right Close-up of a 474th TFW F-16A refuelling from a KC-135 of the 22nd Air Refuelling Wing, which is part of the 15th Air Force (SAC) and is based at March AFB, California (*Frank B Mormillo*)

Left A pleasing study of another 474th TFW
F-16A off the wingtip of the 22nd AREFW
KC-135. The blue fin-stripe on this aircraft
indicates that it was part of the 428th TFS,
one of three squadrons within the 474th.
The small white emblem within the stripe is
a skull and crossbones (*Frank B Mormillo*)

Above Pre-taxy checks are carried out on a
430th TFS/474th TFW F-16A, serial 79–0403,
during a visit to RAF Bentwaters in 1982.
The wing insignia on the intake duct is
noteworthy, as is the fact that the ladder
required for cockpit access is ground
support equipment (GSE). This decision
was clearly taken to save weight, in contrast
to the F-15 and F/A-18 which both have neat
ladders stowed inside the airframe
(*T Malcolm English*)

Below The 'WA' tail-code on this F-16C stands for the USAF Tactical Fighter Weapons Center (TFWC), but the aircraft (83–1129) is assigned to the 57th TFW. It appears to be painted in some variation of the 'lizard' or European One camouflage scheme applied to aircraft such as the A-10, and consisting of dark olive green (FS 34103), dark green (FS 34092) and dark grey (FS 34081). Mounted to the centreline of this aircraft is a Westinghouse AN/ALQ-131 electronic countermeasures pod, this

device giving the F-16 a powerful jamming capability. Photographed at NAS Fallon, Nevada, in September 1988, the 57th TFW aircraft were temporarily based at the air station whilst exercising on the extensive electronic warfare range. The TFWC and 57th TFW are based at Nellis AFB in Nevada, an airfield opened in 1947 and named after First Lt William H Nellis, a P-47 Thunderbolt pilot who died in action in Europe in 1944 (*Paul Bigelow via Bob Archer*)

Left This US Navy F-16N of VF-45 'Blackbirds' is normally based at NAS Key West in Florida, but was photographed landing at NAS Oceana in Virginia in 1989. Its fin bears a Soviet-style red star and the 'AD' tail-code for shore-based aircraft at either of these airfields, or NAS Cecil Field. Its nose carries '21' in the form of a Soviet Bort Number. This is one of a batch of 26 F-16Ns delivered to the Navy between June 1987 and May 1988 for use by adversary squadrons. The F-16N differs from the early production F-16C mainly in having the 28,982 lb (13,600 kg) General Electric F110 engine, a strengthened wing, no gun, and the lighter Westinghouse APG-66 radar in place of the later APG-68. This example is carrying an ACMI data pod on the left wingtip (*Peter R Foster*)

'Red 31' is an F-16N from VF-43
'Challengers', based at NAS Oceana. It
appears to be carrying on station 5R a
sensor similar to the Northrop TCS
(television camera set) for long-range target
identification in air combat training
(*Milslides via Bob Archer*)

One rare bird is this US Marine Corps F-16N (BuNo 163269) photographed in Canada in 1990. The photographer's notes indicate that it came from NFWS (Navy Fighter Weapons School) or 'Top Gun' at NAS Miramar, California, where the F-16N is flown by both this unit and VF-126 'Bandits' (*Robbie Shaw*)

Left A pre-production aircraft at the final assembly stage at General Dynamics' Fort Worth factory (USAF Plant No 4). Despite the many innovations introduced with the F-16, construction is largely traditional, with advanced composite materials restricted to the skins of the tail surfaces. The plant has the capacity to produce 45 F-16s per month, but in a wartime environment this figure could be increased to 200 per month by subcontracting, this rate then being limited by flightline facilities. During World War 2, this factory produced a record 217 B-24s in a 30-day period in 1944. Unlike most aircraft manufacturers, GD has progressed to smaller and smaller aircraft, from the massive 10-engined B-36 to the four-engined supersonic B-58, the twin-engined F-111, and finally to the single-engined F-16 (*USAF*)

Above A pleasant study of the first prototype YF-16 (72-01567) at the Air Force Flight Test Center at Edwards AFB, California, in September 1974, only a few months after its first flight (*Chris Pocock via Bob Archer*)

This F-16A (serial 75–0749) was the fifth of six full-scale development single-seaters, photographed during a visit to RAF Alconbury in May 1979. One obvious change from the YF-16 is that the nose has been enlarged to accommodate the Westinghouse APG-66 radar. Note the use of a single grey paint, and the old-fashioned canards of the AIM-9J-series Sidewinders. Four FSD Fighting Falcons were sent across to Europe to conduct 'in theatre' operations with USAFE units that would eventually receive F-16s en masse in the 1980s (*Bob Archer*)

This early production F-16A (serial 79–0402) was seen at Hill AFB, Utah, in 1987 when it was assigned to the Ogden Air Logistics Center, which provides logistical support on various missiles, including Maverick and 'smart' bombs. Its high-visibility paint scheme suggests that it may have been used in weapons trials. In the background is a standard production F-16 from the 4th TFS (note the black lightning on the yellow stripe) of the 388th TFW (*Milslides via Bob Archer*)

Below A member of the USAF Air Demonstration Squadron or Thunderbirds, photographed at Perth Airport in Western Australia in October 1987. Before the F-16A, the squadron operated (in chronological order) the F-84, F-100, F-105, F-4 and T-38. The change from the T-38 took place in 1982, following a crash in January of that year, in which four pilots and their aircraft were lost. The F-16A was selected to replace the T-38 two months later, and the first public demonstration by these new Thunderbirds took place on 12 March 1983 at their home base of Nellis AFB, Nevada (*Tony Holmes*)

Right Having all arrived safely after a long ferry flight down from Indonesia, the Thunderbirds repose on the Perth International Airport hardstand awaiting attention from the groundcrews. The day before this photo was taken, the team had performed in Jakarta in front of over two million people. Suitably impressed by the display, the Indonesian government ordered 12 F-16s soon afterwards. Compared to the T-38, the F-16A provides a number of improvements in the air display context, including a far greater ferry range, allowing the team to demonstrate overseas more easily than in the past. Comparing maximum turn rates at 330 knots (610 km/hr) at sea level, the F-16A offers an 80 per cent improvement, from 13.5 to 24.5 degrees per second. Despite its larger size and higher thrust/weight ratio, the F-16A burns less than 30 per cent more fuel than the T-38, the average consumption rising from 1400 lbs/hr (635 kgs/hr) to 1800 lbs/hr (815 kgs/hr). The fact that the F-16A has the lowest wing loading of the series makes it especially well suited to the demonstration role (*Tony Holmes*)

Left Close-up of Thunderbird No 4 at the RAF Upper Heyford air display, one of many stops in the team's 1984 European tour (*T Malcolm English*)

Above Dark clouds provide a contrasting backdrop for Thunderbird No 1 at Perth in 1987. Soon to perform in the team's first ever air display in Australia, the F-16 is being readied by its dedicated groundcrew, each of whom has been hand picked for the job (*Tony Holmes*)

Above Six Thunderbirds in perfect formation, showing the black stylized Indian 'Thunderbird' painted on their undersides (*Frank B Mormillo*)

Right The special paint-job accentuates the forebody chine of the F-16A. These strakes serve two aerodynamic purposes, the front half improving directional stability and the rear half delaying flow separation on the wing. According to GD, these surfaces, which were first exploited on the Lockheed SR-71 family, quadruple the lift increment due to the trailing edge flap (*Steve Mansfield*)

This sequence of photographs was taken as the Thunderbirds displayed during the Reno Air Races of 1988 (*Steve Mansfield*)

Above Four Thunderbirds in tight diamond formation with three smoking. The F-16As used by the team differ little from standard production aircraft, aside from their paint scheme and the fact that the M61 cannon is deleted to make space for the tank to store the oil that is injected into the jet to produce the smoke (*Frank B Mormillo*)

Above right Four Thunderbirds make a slow speed flypast, while a fifth overtakes at high speed. Aside from their display duties, the pilots are required to remain proficient in air combat and air-to-surface tactics. In an emergency these colourful aircraft could be repainted and restored to combat configuration within 72 hours. The unit would then become part of the 430th TFS, which in turn is part of the 57th FWW at Nellis AFB (*Duncan Cubitt/Airforces Monthly*)

Below right Two smoking Thunderbirds make a 'mirror pass' at the '88 Reno Air Races, with No 6 erect and No 5 inverted. Note that the latter has its number painted upside-down (*Steve Mansfield*)

Weekend Warriors

In times of crisis and actual conflict, the USAF is supported by well-equipped units of the Air National Guard (ANG) and Air Force Reserve (AFRES), many of which now have the F-16. At the end of 1990, the ANG listed 19 Fighting Falcon units, that force having grown by five in 1989 and a further five in 1990, while the AFRES also had five F-16 units. The following ANG units equipped with the F-16A/B are currently assigned to CONUS air defence in association with TAC:

144th FIW at Fresno Air Terminal, California
107th FIG at Niagara Falls International Airport, New York
119th FIG at Fargo (Hector Field), North Dakota
120th FIG at Great Falls International Airport, Montana
125th FIG at Jacksonville International Airport, Florida
147th FIG at Ellington Field AGS, Texas
148th FIG at Duluth International Airport, Minnesota
158th FIG at Burlington International Airport, Vermont
177th FIG at Atlantic City International Airport, New Jersey
191st FIG at Selfridge ANGB, Michigan.

In addition, the following ANG units are assigned to TAC in the tactical fighter role, which includes ground attack duties:

113th TFW at Andrews AFB, Maryland
127th TFW at Selfridge ANGB, Michigan
174th TFW at Syracuse (Hancock Field), New York
149th TFG at Kelly AFB, Texas
169th TFG at McEntire ANGB, South Carolina
183rd TFG at Springfield Capital Airport, Illinois
184th TFG at McConnell AFB, Kansas
187th TFG at Montgomery (Dannelly Field), Alabama
188th TFG at Fort Smith Municipal Airport, Arkansas.

The F-16A/B is also operated by the 114th TFTS of the 142nd FIG at Kingsley Field in Oregon, providing air defence training. Fighter assets of AFRES are concentrated in the 10th Air Force, headquartered at Bergstrom AFB, Texas. The units currently equipped with the F-16 are as follows:

419th TFW at Hill AFB, Utah
482nd TFW at Homestead AFB, Florida
507th TFG at Tinker AFB, Oklahoma
906th TFG at Wright-Patterson AFB, Ohio.
944th TFG at Luke AFB, Arizona

It may be noted that the 944th TFG appears to be the only AFRES (or ANG) unit equipped with the F-16C/D. Also that AFRES training has included reservists from the 419th TFW deploying their F-16A/Bs to Denmark in 1988.

Previous pages An interesting line-up of Falcon tail feathers at London, Ontario in June 1990. Those identifiable in this shot include F-16A 80–0505 from the 191st FIG of the Michigan ANG (distinguished from the 12th TFW by the chequered stripe), F-16A 78–0069 from the 162nd TFG of the Arizona ANG (which provides training for both the A-7 and F-16), F-16A 80–0495 and F-16B 80–0624 from the 184th TFG of the Kansas ANG, F-16A 82–0944 from the 31st TTW at Homestead AFB, Florida, and F-16A 82–0985 from the 3246th Test Wing at Eglin AFB, Florida (*Robbie Shaw*)

Above The 'DC' tail-code is for the 113th TFW of the Maryland ANG, and the black fin stripe with four white stars denotes the 121st TFS. The aircraft being escorted (83–4615) is a Boeing C-22B, one of four such 727-series operated by the HQ-ANG Bureau (Eastern Division). Both aircraft are based at Andrews AFB, some 11 miles (17.6 km) from Washington DC. The base was activated in 1943, and was named after Lt Gen Frank M Andrews, a military aviation pioneer and a World War 2 commander in the European theatre who died in a flying accident in Iceland in 1943 (*Robert F Dorr*)

Right The only ANG unit to have the President of the United States as both its state and Federal Commander-in-Chief, the 121st TFS has always prided itself on its long fighter lineage. Initially formed in April 1941 as an observation squadron flying Piper L-4s and Stinson L-5s, the 121st traded up to P-47Ds in 1946. F-84s, F-94s, F-51Hs, F-86s and F-100s followed over the next three decades, the venerable Super Sabres eventually being replaced by equally veteran F-105s in 1975. Flown to Davis-Monthan AFB in 1981, the Thunderchiefs then made way for F-4Cs, these Vietnam vets finally earning an honourable retirement when the first of 15 F-16As arrived in late 1989 (*Robert F Dorr*)

Although the 142nd FIG of the Oregon
ANG is primarily an F-15A/B air defence
training unit, it includes the 114th TFTS
equipped with F-16A/Bs such as this
example (81–0811). The air defence fin flash
for the 142nd FIG is described formally as a
red hawk, but for the F-16s it is toned
down. The unit is based at Portland
International Airport (*Robbie Shaw*)

This attractive portrait of F-16A, 80–0607 was taken as it climbed out from Tucson International Airport, which serves as base for the Arizona ANG's 162nd TFG. This squadron functions as a Replacement Training Unit (RTU) for the A-7D/K Corsair II and the F-16A/B, the latter aircraft being operated as the 148 TFTS (*Peter R Foster*)

Right Bad time for a flame-out! That same F-16A on the approach to Tucson International in October 1988 (*Peter R Foster*)

Above That self-same F-16A of the Arizona ANG, flying over some of that state's less than hospitable real estate. The 148th TFTS includes in its number ten F-16A/Bs that belong to the Royal Netherlands Air Force, these aircraft being used by ANG instructors to train Dutch pilots in the art of flying the Fighting Falcon. The F-16s bear serials in the range 88–0219 to 88–0269 and the same ANG markings as the other aircraft (*Peter R Foster*)

Above One unusual feature of 159th FIS aircraft, as illustrated here by 80–0608, is that they have individual numbers that bear no relation to their serials. In this case the number is '05', and it appears both on the rear fuselage and the nosewheel door. Note the relatively advanced AIM-9L front end on the Sidewinder acquisition round (*Paul F Crickmore*)

Right The Florida ANG's 125th FIG is an air defence unit with a fin flash that is formally described as a blue/white lightning bolt, although (as this 1990 photograph shows) this marking has recently been toned down. These three F-16As (81–0757, 80–0608 and 81–0681) are part of the group's 159th FIS, this unit being based at Jacksonville International Airport (*Paul F Crickmore*)

Overleaf The same trio from the 159th TFS in echelon port, with ACMI data pods on the left wingtips and AIM-9L acquisition rounds (with individual letters on the wings) on the right (*Paul F Crickmore*)

Below This F-16B (serial 81–0818) is one of two currently operated by the 159th TFS of the 125th FIG, photographed at Jacksonville (*Milslides via Bob Archer*)

Right The 120th FIG of the Montana ANG is an air defence unit, based at Great Falls International Airport. This F-16A (serial 80–0563) from the 186th FIS was photographed refuelling from a KC-135E close to the Mexican border. Note the additional Sidewinder rails on stations two and eight (*Peter R Foster*)

Four F-16Cs from the AFRES 944th TFG's 302nd TFS start their landing break. The unit is based at Luke AFB, Arizona (*Dave Donald*)

Above These F-16As from the 186th FIS (serials 82–1023 and 81–0666) were photographed making a slow pass at the 1988 Reno Air Races. In addition to the fin-stripe, the unit's aircraft are painted with a buffalo's head superimposed on an outline of Montana hills. At the base of the fin is painted the legend 'Big Sky Country' (*Steve Mansfield*)

Right Close-up of the 944th's F-16C serial 86–0214, illustrating the unit's 'LR' tail-code, the yellow fin-stripe with a red trident, and the small red devil below the stripe. Note the unit badge on the intake plug (*Peter R Foster*)

European Flavour

The very early history of the F-16 has been discussed in Chapter One, to the point where this aircraft was selected by the USAF as its new air combat fighter on 13 January 1975. The F-16 had thus passed its first crucial test, but it then became a matter of convincing some of the principal European air forces to adopt the aircraft in what became known as 'The Sale of the Century'. If successful, this effort would reduce the USAF's programme costs, provide more work for GD, and improve equipment standardization within NATO.

To show the aircraft to representatives of European air forces, one of the YF-16 prototypes was flown to Europe for the 1975 Paris Airshow, where it staggered the crowds with its remarkable manoeuvrability. On 7 June 1975 it was formally announced that the F-16 had been adopted by the services of Belgium, Denmark, the Netherlands and Norway, with each of these nations taking part in a co-production programme with final assembly lines in Belgium and Holland. These four nations were designated as the European Participating Group (EPG), and the initial plan was that they would purchase 348 F-16s, made up of 116 for Belgium, 58 for Denmark, 102 for the Netherlands and 72 for Norway. At time of writing, 147 have been delivered to Belgium, 70 to Denmark, 194 to the Netherlands, and 74 to Norway, giving a total of 485 aircraft. On present plans, Belgium will increase its procurement to 160 and the Netherlands to 213, giving an eventual total of 517 F-16s. However, there may be much more F-16 work for the local aerospace industry if the EPG decides to go along with GD proposals for an 'Agile Falcon' with a much larger wing and later equipment.

Left The Royal Danish Air Force (*Kongelige Danske Flivevabnet*) has purchased a total of 67 F-16A/Bs, which are assigned to the air defence role and are operated as four squadrons: *Eskadrilles* 723 and 726 at Aalborg; and *Esk* 727 and 730 at Skrydstrup. The aircraft are painted in standard USAF camouflage, and bear miniature Danish markings. This photograph shows the toned-down serial (E-602, ex 80–3602, c/n 6F-37, and a member of *Esk* 730) and the carriage of a dayglo red dummy AIM-9J on the left tip and a -9L acquisition round on the right (*Ian Black*)

Below Another member of *Esk* 730, E-174 maintains close formation with an RAF Tornado F.3, the F-16 carrying the almost mandatory AIM-9L acquisition round on its starboard rail (*Ian Black*)

Right Danish F-16A serial E-192 (ex 78–0192, c/n 6F-19) is assigned to *Esk* 730 at Skrydstrup, but was pictured on this occasion in formation with another Tornado F.3 (serial ZE791/FF) from No 25 Sqn at Leeming. It may be noted that the air defence Tornado's 'flint grey' is significantly lighter than the greys of the F-16 (*Ian Black*)

Left An unusual view of F-16A serial E-600 (ex 80–3600, c/n 6F-35) from *Esk* 723 at Aalborg. The use of dayglo colours on the Sidewinders reduces the risk of collisions during formation flying, but is probably unique to Denmark (*Ian Black*)

Above An unidentified Danish F-16A in typical one-tank, two-missile configuration. In some respects the F-16A/Bs of the four EPAF services have been left behind by the F-16C/D series, but this situation may be rectified around the turn of the century by modifying these older aircraft to take larger wings and more advanced avionics (*Ian Black*)

Above Danish F-16A serial E-199 (ex 78–0199, c/n 6F–26) from *Esk* 727 at Skrydstrup, making a slow speed pass with airbrakes open, at the 1988 Mildenhall Air Fete (*T Malcolm English*)

Right One of 14 F-16Bs flown by the RDAF, illustrating the leading edge flap, which is drooped automatically to give the optimum turn rate in combat (*Ian Black*)

Above One photograph that gives the expression 'down amongst the weeds' a whole new meaning. This F-16A (serial E-596 ex 80–3596, c/n 6F-31, *Esk* 723) was photographed at dispersal at Aalborg in 1985 (*Peter R Foster*)

Right The front cockpit of a Danish F-16B, with the sidestick controller clearly visible on the right-hand shelf. Radar information appears on the multi-function display on the left of the up-front controls, which in turn are just below the GEC Avionics HUD. The cockpit is relatively small by American standards, and features a semi-reclined seat to increase the pilot's G-tolerance (*Ian Black*)

Left Another two-seater, this time ET-614 (ex 80–3614, c/n 6G-11) of *Esk* 727. Although Denmark does not have its own F-16 assembly line, nine Danish companies are involved in work for the co-production programme (*Ian Black*)

Above The Belgian Air Force, known in-country as the *Force Aérienne Belge* or the *Belgische Luchtmacht*, purchased its Fighting Falcons in two batches. The initial order covered 116 F-16A/Bs, the first of which was delivered in January 1979 and the last in 1985. These aircraft replaced the F-104G Starfighter, and formed No 1 Wing at Beauvechain, with Nos 349 and 350 Sqn, and No 10 Wing at Kleine Brogel, with Nos 23 and 31 Sqn. A further 44 F-16A/Bs was ordered to replace the Mirage, with deliveries beginning in 1987 to form No 2 Wing at Florennes, with Nos 1 and 2 Sqn. The total of 160 provides 136 F-16As and 24 F-16Bs. One example of either type appears in this line-up (*Ian Black*)

Left A well-composed shot of a classic strafing target, recorded in 1988 at Beauvechain airbase (*Ian Black*)

Above Belgian F-16A serial FA-21 (ex 78–0136, c/n 6H-21), a representative of No 349 *Smaldeel* (Sqn) of No I *Bevekom* (Wing), seen at RAF Waddington during the 1988 Tactical Fighter Meet. The well-worn fin-stripe contains only vestiges of the No 349 Sqn badge, referred to as 'Goedendag', or crossed clubs in a circle. Its serial implies an early delivery, suggesting Block 01 production standard. Its age is also to be seen in the small, unclipped tailplane, the current design having been introduced with Block 15, starting at the end of 1981 as the result of engineering change proposal (ECP) 425. The larger tail with a clipped tip for ground clearance was brought in to increase pitch control authority and overcome a superstall problem. With the original tail it was possible to overshoot the 25 degree AOA limit and enter a deep stall, from which recovery was possible only by a special technique (*T Malcolm English*)

Above This side elevation of the pilot of F-16A serial FA-75 illustrates how high he is placed in the cockpit, with his knees above the sill-line. Should the canopy be lost in flight, some blast protection is nonetheless provided by the glare shield and HUD (*Ian Black*)

Right In head-on view the devil's head on the pilot's bone-dome confirms that FA-75 (ex 80–3566, c/n 6H-75) is assigned to No 23 Sqn of No 1 Wing at Beauvechain. One of the problems associated with the semi-reclined seat is that pilots' find it more difficult to turn round and 'check six', but the problem is eased by using the 'towel rack' handles and a special head movement. Some pilots also complain that it is difficult to enter the F-16 gracefully, but the seat inclination (30 degrees, compared to the usual 13) does produce a more comfortable cockpit (*Ian Black*)

Above A winter's scene, not at Kleine Brogel where this F-16B (serial FB-13 ex 80–3588, c/n 6J-13) is based with No 10 Wing, but at the Canadian Forces base at Baden Söllingen in Germany, in November 1988 (*Bob Archer*)

Above right The tiger badge of these four F-16As in echelon starboard indicates No 31 Sqn, hence the rampart lion represents the insignia of No 10 Wing at Kleine Brogel. The picture was taken in 1987, and it is surprising that three of the pilots were still wearing high visibility white bone-domes at this late stage, these helmets showing up almost as well as the glint on the afterburner nozzles (*Peter R Foster*)

Below right Another example of No 31 Sqn equipment, F-16A serial FA-94 (ex 80–3585, c/n 6H-94) is seen landing at RAF Mildenhall in 1988 (*Duncan Cubitt/Airforces Monthly*)

Above Someone appears to have gone overboard with No 31 Sqn's tiger insignia! The scheme was specially applied to this F-16 to celebrate the squadron's hosting of the 1985 Tiger Meet at Kleine Brogel, the aircraft being transformed by a coat of latex. Prior to the stripes being applied, seven coats of primer paint had to be sprayed onto the F-16 to protect the aircraft's expensive anti-radar scheme.

Only one flight was made in the gaudy Falcon, a Capt Marc Libaers taking the aircraft aloft on 5 July 1985. The forward section of the aircraft remained unpainted for safety reasons as the F16 shed its stripes in large chunks during its solitary flight. The scheme itself cost $US 1300, the squadron footing the bill from its own funds (*Ian Black*)

Right This F-16B (serial FB-11 ex 78–0172, c/n 6J-11) was pictured outside a HAS at RAF Wattisham in 1986. It came from No 1 Wing at Beauvechain, and is now thought to be assigned to No 350 Sqn, though it lacks the 'Ambiorix' Viking's head insignia of that unit (*Bob Archer*)

Above left The first two-seater produced for Belgium, FB-01 (ex 78–0162, c/n 6J-1) was photographed at Brustem in 1989, its colours celebrating the 10th anniversary of the F-16's entry into service with the BAF. The squadron badges are painted on the fin leading edge: from top to bottom, the crossed clubs of No 349 Sqn; the Viking's head of No 350 Sqn; the devil's head of No 23 Sqn; the tiger's head of No 31 Sqn; and the badges of No 2 Wing's two units, Nos 1 and 2 Sqns. The insignia at the top of the fin is that of the BAF's Tactical Air Force Command (TAFC). The records indicate that FB-01 is currently assigned to No 31 Sqn (*Bob Archer*)

Below left The Royal Norwegian Air Force (*Kongelige Norske Luftforsvaret*) began taking delivery of the F-16A/B in January 1980, and later ordered two more F-16Bs to supplement the original batch of 72 F-16A/Bs. The Falcons are operated as four squadrons at three bases: Nos 331 and 334 at Bodo in the north; No 332 at Rygge in the south; and No 338 at Orland, mid-way between these airfields. The F-16A/B is employed in both the air defence and anti-shipping strike roles (the latter with the Penguin Mk 3 missile), and for this reason it differs from other EPAF Falcons in being painted overall in middle grey (FS 36118). It also differs in having a 23 ft (7.0 m) ribbon parachute, which involves a weight penalty of 163 lbs (74 kgs), but reduces ground roll on icy runways by around 57 per cent. This example of the Norwegian F-16A appears set to roll on a typically inclement day at RAF Brawdy (*John Dibbs*)

Above This Norwegian F-16A (serial 298, ex 78–0298, c/n 6K–27) was photographed in Belgium at Liège-Bierset in 1986. The serial numbers run from 272 to 307 and from 658 to 688. This aircraft is reportedly allocated to No 338 Sqn at Orland, and the yellow lightning flash in a black triangle is that unit's badge (*H Barnich via Bob Archer*)

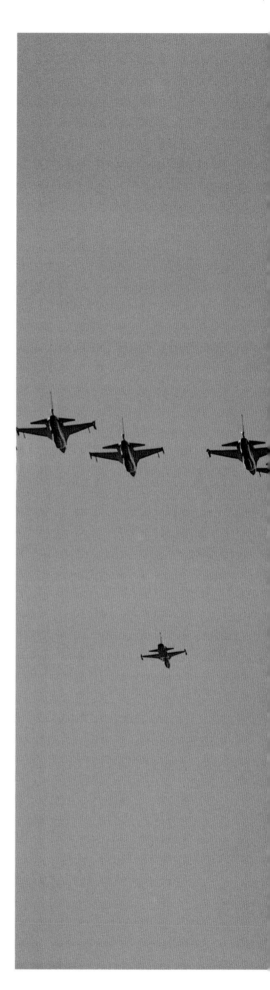

Right A massed fly-past of F-16A/Bs, mixed in with F-5As, cruises over Klanten in Norway during RNAF celebrations in 1989. Interestingly, some Falcons carry wing tanks whilst others don't, the tanked F-16s having flown in from bases in northern Norway (*Duncan Cubitt/Airforces Monthly*)

Above The Royal Netherlands Air Force (*Koninklijke Luchtmacht*) has ordered a total of 213 F-16A/Bs to replace both the F-104G and NF-5. By the end of 1991 these Falcons will form eight squadrons at four bases. The Leeuwarden wing was the first to receive the F-16A/B, with deliveries beginning in June 1979, and No 322 Sqn was declared operational in May 1981. No 323 Sqn at the same base followed in April 1982, and retains a conversion training supplementary role. This was followed by the Volkel wing, with all three squadrons converted by the end of 1985. Nos 311 and 312 Sqns are allocated to the strike role, and No 306 Sqn will perform tactical reconnaissance until 1993. At Twenthe the F-16 replaced the NF-5 at No 315 Sqn in 1988, and with No 313 Sqn in 1990. The final squadron to convert is No 314 at Gilze-Rijen, which will be operational with the F-16 by the end of 1991. Dutch military aircraft are identified by a letter code ('J' for the F-16, 'K' for the NF-5 and 'D' for the F-104G) and three digits reflecting the construction number of previous identity. This example, serial J-231, was formerly 78–0231 (construction number 6D-20), and its badge is an Amazonian archer in a black circle, indicating No 323 Sqn at Leeuwarden (*Ian Black*)

Left Another member of No 323 Sqn is this F-16B, serial J-270 (formerly 78–0270, c/n 6E-12), photographed tanking up in 1985 from a KC-135 (*Robbie Shaw*)

Above Two representatives of No 323 Sqn provide side elevation and plan views of the F-16 in company with RAF Lightning F.6 (serial XR754/BC) from No 11 Sqn this veteran British fighter now spending its days with the Battle Damage Repair Training Unit at Honington. This F-16B was the first two-seater for the Netherlands, serial J-259 being derived from its earlier USAF serial 78–0259, while its c/n was 6E-1 (*Ian Black*)

Below This close-up of a No 323 Sqn F-16A (hopefully taken with a telephoto lens) illustrates the proximity of the GEC Avionics HUD to the transparency. Probably the most unusual development in the cockpit display business, this HUD not only corrects for optical distortion in weapon aiming, but also protects the pilot from the travelling wave produced in the hood by bird impact. Without this specially strengthened HUD, the pilot was liable to be knocked unconscious by the indentation created by the bird. The F-16's use of a combined hood and windscreen (eliminating the usual framework) did wonders for visibility, but introduced a whole host of unforeseen problems. Because the whole transparency has to be thick enough to withstand a bird strike, it is too heavy to eject through, hence three separate systems have to be provided for hood jettison. The lack of framework can be disorientating, and the sheer thickness of the hood appears to give problems with reflections when flying at night. Interestingly, Mitsubishi, have gone back to a separate windscreen for the proposed FS-X attack derivative of the F-16 (*Ian Black*)

Left The same No 323 Sqn aircraft, but this time viewed from a safer distance. The ventral intake provides some protection for the engine against flow distortion caused by high AOA operation, and (according to GD) is higher off the ground (in height/diameter terms) than the intakes of a 737. At the preliminary design stage the inlet face was much further forward, then it was cut back to save weight, the rear limit probably being decided by the need for a reasonable wheel-base, in this case 13.1 ft (3.99 m) (*Ian Black*)

Above left Another No 323 Sqn F-16A
landing at RAF Alconbury in 1988. Before it
was J-254 it was allocated the US serial
78–0254, and its construction number was
6D-43, indicating that it was the 43rd
single-seater built for the Netherlands
(*Peter R Foster*)

Below left A pleasing landing shot of one of
No 323's two-seaters, serial J-259,
decorated to celebrate the 10th anniversary
of F-16 operations at Leeuwarden
(*John Dibbs*)

Above This F-16A(R), (serial J-635, formerly
80–3635, c/n 6D-67), belongs to No 306 Sqn,
the dedicated photo-recce unit. The
cylindrical centre-line store is clearly
different in shape from the standard fuel
tank, and may be the Odelft Orpheus
reconnaissance pod, which is used only by
No 306 Sqn. The pod contains one forward
and four lateral oblique cameras with focal
lengths in the 70–150 mm range, an infra-
red linescan (IRLS) and its own
environmental control system. Flight trials
were carried out in 1980–81, and the first
production delivery took place in February
1983. The pod is 148 inches (3.76 m) long,
has a diameter of 18.5 inches (47 cm), and
weighs 1272 lbs (577 kgs). Internally, the
F-16A(R)s have a specially modified radar
altimeter and control box to allow the pilot
to operate the Orpheus system. The recce –
F-16s are due to be modified in the early
1990s into laser-designator aircraft, thus
losing their photographic role altogether
(*Ian Black*)

Right No 315 Sqn's F-16B serial J-065 is a later production model, as evidenced by the larger, clipped tailplane. The unusual afterburner effect makes the aircraft look as though it is powered by two rocket engines, and the large manoeuvre flaps stand out very clearly. These flaps have a maximum depression of 25 degrees, but can be raised through 2.5 degrees to eliminate the wing's basic camber in high speed flight. The flaps are also raised during the take-off run to minimize drag and eliminate the nose-down pitching movement they would produce in the undeflected position. At rotation a micro-switch on the nose gear moves the flap down, and they are then programmed for Mach number and AOA. By the time the aircraft has reached Mach 0.99 in level flight, the flap is raised 2.5 degrees again. This photograph was taken at Mildenhall Air Fête in 1989 (*Duncan Cubitt/Airforces Monthly*)

Above Dutch Falcons ready to roll. The F-16A (J-710) bears the No 315 Sqn badge of a yellow lion's head in a blue circle (*Ian Black*)

Left Dutch F-16A J-516 (from No 315 Sqn), as demonstrated at Farnborough in 1990, with Sanders' 'Smokewinders' on the wingtips to make this small aircraft more visible to the spectators and to dramatize its manoeuvres and attitudes. At this point the Falcon was clearly close to its maximum AOA of 25 degrees. The aircraft was flown alternately by Steve Barter, chief experimental test pilot for GD, and Bland Smith, one of Barter's team (*Dave Donald*)

Above Heading for that wild blue yonder, F-16A serial J-061 shows the No 315 Sqn badge in toned-down form, although the fin-stripe remains in full colour. The widely advertised 9G capability of the F-16A is available in sustained form only at low altitude at speeds around Mach 0.8–0.9, but it can be attained instantaneously at heights up to 36,000 ft (11,000 m) and speeds up to Mach 2.05. These figures relate to an F-16A with two AIM-9s, 511 rounds for the M61, and half internal fuel (*John Dibbs*)

Left A colourful ending for this Dutch F-16A from No 315 Sqn, as presented at Mildenhall Air Fête in May 1990. The airbrakes are open their full 60 degrees, and the braking parachute is clearly visible. In the background are the even more colourful Alpha Jets of the *Patrouille de France* (*T Malcolm English*)

Above A dramatic shot of that same aircraft (serial J-060) being hauled off the ground, with undercarriage doors still closing and 'Smokewinders' already smoking. This F-16A from No 315 Sqn was the 1990 display aircraft for the Royal Netherlands Air Force (*John Blackman*)

Right Frank Sanders' smoke pods are used to good effect as the Dutch pilot cranks on the full 25 degrees AOA. Frank died in a T-33 crash in New Mexico in 1990, but his son Dennis is continuing the business (*T Malcolm English*)

Above Same aeroplane, different event. Photographed two months later at RAF Brawdy in Wales, J-060 was almost a permanent fixture at British airshows throughout 1990, its stunning routine never failing to impress the crowds (*Robbie Shaw*)

Photographed in 1988, this F-16A (J-864) from No 312 Sqn had been extensively decorated to celebrate the 75th anniversary of the Royal Netherlands Air Force, which was established in 1913 as an army corps. As shown here, the squadron badge (crossed swords and a red lightning flash in a black circle) is normally carried on the fin, but in the case of this display aircraft it has been moved to the ventral fins. The Alouette III (A-529) is one of a large number operated by the service in the form of two squadrons: No 298 at Soesterberg and No 300 at Deelen, where this photograph was taken (*Robbie Shaw*)

A standard production F-16A (J-864) of No 312 Sqn, pictured at RAF Coningsby in 1985. The wingtip Sidewinder rails are a permanent fit, used (as in the case of the F-5) as an anti-flutter mass. The pilot's toned-down bone-dome is well illustrated in this view, this essential item of clothing contrasting markedly with the high-visibility helmets worn by Dutch pilots in the early 1980s (*Peter R Foster*)

Right The No 312 Sqn pilot of F-16A serial J-877 throttles back, pulls up the nose and stands on the brakes in this 1987 photograph (*John Blackman*)

Above This F-16B, from No 312 Sqn, was photographed landing at Nellis AFB in 1984 after a Red Flag sortie. When the purse strings allow it, the Dutch usually send a squadron of F-16s to Nellis to fly and fight in an environment not available to them in Europe (*Frank B Mormillo*)

Above Turkey's selection of the F-16 led to the establishing of the fourth Fighting Falcon production line, which assembled all but the first eight F-16 C/Ds in the 160-aircraft *Peace Onyx* programme. Airbrakes open and about to touch down at Ankara-Mürted in 1990, this F-16C (89–0022) is a member of the Turkish Air Force's No 4 Wing. The service received its first Fighting Falcon in July 1987 (*Robbie Shaw*)

Above right Another F-16C (86–0068) of No 4 Wing at Mürted in September 1990. At this base the F-16 replaces two Starfighter squadrons: No 141, which previously had the F-104G, and No 142, which had the F-104S. The Turkish order consists of 128 F-16Cs and 32 F-16Ds, of which 152 are being assembled by Tusas Aerospace Industries (TAI), which is 42 per cent owned by GD and seven per cent by GE. The company was formed in May 1984, and the first Turkish assembled aircraft was delivered in November 1987. By the end of 1990 over 70 F-16s had been delivered (*Robbie Shaw*)

Below right An example of the two-seat F-16D (88–0013), another Block 30 aircraft of the 4th Wing. Most 'twin tubs' are flown by *Oncel Filo*, the Turkish Air Force Falcon OCU at Murted. Only high-time fighter pilots are currently being chosen to fly F-16s in the Turkish Air Force, many ex Starfighter and Phantom II 'jocks' now tackling their NATO allies with confidence in the skies over Mürted and Bandirma (*Robbie Shaw*)

Falcon Exotica

As described in the previous chapter, production of the F-16 at GD's plant at Fort Worth, Texas, Fokker in Holland and SABCA in Belgium, was launched on the basis of a planned procurement by the USAF (initially for 650 aircraft) and by the EPG nations for a further 348, giving a prospective total of almost 1000 F-16s at the outset. However, the initial batch was a comparatively modest 352 aircraft, covering 105 for the USAF, 192 for the EPAF, and 55 for Iran (out of a planned 160). The Iranian deal fell through in January 1979, but by August 1977 Israel had announced the intention to order 75 F-16A/Bs, and other overseas orders began to pour in.

At time of writing Israel has taken delivery of 75 F-16A/Bs and 75 F-16C/Ds, and a further 60 are planned; Egypt has received 41 F-16A/Bs and 40 F-16C/Ds, and plans a further 40; Pakistan has 40 F-16A/Bs, but plans to buy 71 additional aircraft; Venezuela has 24 F-16A/Bs; Turkey (where a fourth production line has been established) has 55 F-16C/Ds, but plans a total of 160; Greece has 40 F-16C/Ds; Singapore has 8 F-16A/Bs; Thailand has 12 F-16A/Bs; Indonesia has 12 F-16A/Bs; South Korea has 36 F-16C/Ds; Portugal has 12 refurbished F-16A/Bs; and Bahrain has 10 F-16C/Ds.

The aircraft discussed so far have been standard production F-16s, with relatively small variations in equipment and armament. However, the aircraft's FBW system and its modular construction makes it particularly suited to configurational modifications. For example, in 1975 ventral canards were added to a YF-16, producing the CCV/F-16. The concept was taken further in the Advanced Fighter Technology Integration (AFTI)/F-16, which was based on an FSD aircraft and had triplex digital controls. A far greater change was the F-16XL, which has a fuselage stretch and a cranked arrow wing, an aircraft that is known unofficially as the 'Electric Wedge' (to show the change from the standard 'Electric Jet'). Yet another derivative is the Mitsubishi FS-X, a dedicated attack aircraft for the JASDF, looking rather like the AFTI/F-16, but with Japanese avionics and an enlarged composite wing. With an aircraft as flexible as the F-16, the variations are endless, and the series will clearly continue for many years to come.

Left Nice scenery, but a bad place to eject! Cruising over the Himalayas on a combat patrol near the disputed border with India, this pair of 'Sidewindered' F-16As belong to No 11 'Arrows' Sqn of the Pakistan Air Force (PAF). Tactically based at Sargodha (near Lahore), the F-16s are easily in reach of both the Afghan and Indian borders. Charged with keeping Pakistani airspace clear of intruders, No 11 Sqn has regularly intercepted and shot down stray 'enemy' aircraft over the past seven years (*Peter Steinemann/Skyline APA*)

Rather surprisingly, the standard USAF tactical greys seem to blend in perfectly with the snowy landscape below. Surrounded by potentially hostile air forces who fly MiG-29s and Mirage 2000s amongst other things, the PAF rarely send their F-16s aloft without firstly arming them with live AIM-9s. These Falcons carry a mix of Juliet and Lima model Sidewinders on the wingtip stations
(Peter Steinemann/Skyline APA)

A major user of American hardware in the 1950s and early 60s, Pakistan fell out of favour with the White House after its first war with India in 1965. Utilizing Chinese and French designs for much of the 1970s, Pakistan was once again welcomed into the fold through the commencement of another war – the Soviet invasion of Afghanistan in December 1979. Fearing further communist aggression in this already unstable region, the US approved the sale of 28 F-16As and 12 F-16Bs to the PAF in 1980, the first aircraft arriving in-country in January 1983. Replacing Shenyang F-6s (Chinese MiG-19 copies) as the spearhead of the Air Defence Command, the F-16s currently equip Nos 9 and 11 Sqns, plus an OCU, all of which are based at Sargodha
(*Peter Steinemann/Skyline APA*)

Above left Wearing no distinguishing squadron markings, individual F-16s can only be traced to their units by the USAF-style serial worn on the fin of each aircraft. An impressive line up in peacetime, these 'Arrows' Sqn F-16s could easily be destroyed by a ground hugging Sukhoi Su-22 or Hindustani Jaguar in a pre-emptive strike on the PAF. In light of such opposition, one wonders what the Lee Enfield-toting soldier in the background could do during an attack? He has got his bayonet mounted in anticipation of trouble, however! (*Peter Steinemann/Skyline APA*)

Below left More F-16s have been delivered, or are on order, including some which have the capability to carry the Martin Marietta Lantirn system, or the French-built Thomson-CFS ATLIS-2 laser designator. These bolt-on extras give the PAF a day/night strike capability for the first time since the venerable Martin B-57s were retired from frontline service in 1982. Eleven F-16As, plus 200 AIM-7F Sparrows, were delivered in 1988, whilst the Bush administration agreed the following year to the sale of a further 60 Falcons from 1992 onwards. At least two Falcons have been lost by the PAF; one was reputedly shot down by a Soviet Su-25 *Frogfoot* on 29 April 1987 whilst it attempted to intercept Afghan Su-22s strafing refugee camps near the Pakistani border; and another single seater was 'downed' by a stray wild boar which took a liking to the Sargodha runway on 30 December 1986 (*Peter Steinemann/Skyline APA*)

Above The Republic of Korea Air Force (ROKAF or *Han-guk Kong Goon*) was the first overseas operator to receive the F-16C/D, with deliveries beginning ahead of those for Israel. Between early 1986 and early 1989 a total of 30 F-16Cs and 6 F-16Ds were delivered, and an attrition batch of four aircraft will be delivered in late 1991. This line-up of 87–657, 86–591 and 86–587 appears to suggest that, compared to the standard USAF colour scheme, the dark grey used in the saddle area has been eliminated, producing a much lighter aircraft that is probably better camouflaged for the air-to-air role (*Peter Steinemann/Skyline APA*)

Korean F-16C serial 86–591 touches down,
the carbon deposits around the M61 muzzle
suggesting recent firing practice, and the
background evoking memories of the
MASH television series
(*Peter Steinemann/Skyline APA*)

This ROKAF F-16D bears the serial 85–584 and some of the most toned-down markings ever seen. The South Koreans initially inquired about purchasing 72 F-16As from General Dynamics in the mid 1970s, this request being partly met by the White House in 1978 when they offered 60 aircraft to the Asian nation. However, this agreement was soon downgraded when the Americans replaced the standard Alpha model with the more austere F-16/79. After much political wrangling, a deal was finally struck in 1986 for F-16C/Ds (*Peter Steinemann/Skyline APA*)

Venezuela is the only country in Latin America to operate the F-16. Such nations were expected to purchase the F-16/79 as a modern successor to the F-5E, but Venezuela insisted on the F-16A/B, and more recently some small nations (eg, Bahrain) have successfully insisted on the F-16C/D. This F-16A (7268) from *Grupo de Caza* 16 was pictured landing at Maracay airfield in October 1990 (*Peter R Foster*)

A line-up of F-16A/Bs of the *Fuerzas Aereas Venezolanas* in their readiness shelters, the closest aircraft bearing the serial 5422. Venezuela received six F-16Bs in late 1983 and 18 F-16As during 1985 (*Peter R Foster*)

Fighting Falcon serial 3260, illustrating the
unique Venezuelan camouflage. Equipping
Escuadrones 161 and 162 within *Grupo de
Caza* 16, the F-16s are adorned with
scrambled serials for some unspecified
reason (*Peter R Foster*)